MW00815116

GALAXY OF SUPERSTARS

Ben Affleck

Backstreet Boys

Garth Brooks

Mariah Carey

Cameron Diaz

Leonardo DiCaprio

Tom Hanks

Hanson

Jennifer Love Hewitt

Lauryn Hill

Ewan McGregor

Mike Myers

'N Sync

LeAnn Rimes

Britney Spears

Spice Girls

Jonathan Taylor Thomas

Venus Williams

CHELSEA HOUSE PUBLISHERS

GALAXY OF SUPERSTARS

Jennifer Love Hewitt

Virginia Aronson

CHELSEA HOUSE PUBLISHERS
Philadelphia

Frontis: *At age 20, Jennifer Love Hewitt is already a superstar who has charmed audiences worldwide with her delightful, down-to-earth personality.*

Produced by
21st Century Publishing and Communications, Inc.
New York, New York
http://www.21cpc.com

CHELSEA HOUSE PUBLISHERS

Editor in Chief: Stephen Reginald
Managing Editor: James D. Gallagher
Production Manager: Pamela Loos
Art Director: Sara Davis
Director of Photography: Judy L. Hasday
Senior Production Editor: LeeAnne Gelletly
Publishing Coordinator: James McAvoy
Assistant Editor/Project Editor: Anne Hill
Cover Designer: Emiliano Begnardi

Front Cover Photo: Ron Wolfson/London Features Int'l
Back Cover Photo: Photofest

The Chelsea House World Wide Web address is
http://www.chelseahouse.com

First Printing

1 3 5 7 9 8 6 4 2

Library of Congress Cataloging-in-Publication Data

Aronson, Virginia.
   Jennifer Love Hewitt / Virginia Aronson.
   64 p. cm. – (Galaxy of superstars)
   Filmography: p. 61
   Includes bibliographical references and index.
   Summary: Biography of the Hollywood actress who appeared in a television series at the age of ten and who has since starred in feature films and recorded musical albums.
   ISBN 0-7910-5497-7 (hb.) — ISBN 0-7910-5498-5 (pbk.)
   1. Hewitt, Jennifer Love, 1979–   —Juvenile literature. 2. Motion picture actors and actresses—United States—Biography—Juvenile literature. [1. Hewitt, Jennifer Love, 1979–   . 2. Actors and actresses.] I. Title. II. Series.
PN2287.H476A76 1999
791.43'028'092—dc21
[B]   99—35561
                                                                  CIP
                                                                   AC

CONTENTS

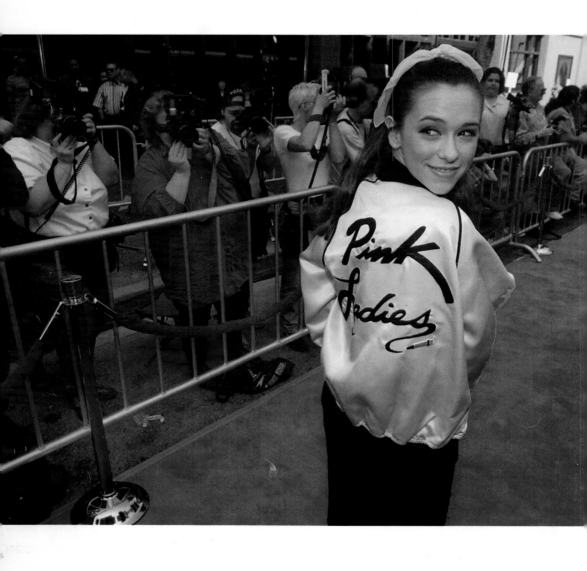

1

DREAMS
OF LOVE

One bright California morning in 1998, Jennifer Love Hewitt awoke suddenly from a dream—a strange and very wonderful dream. There had been a wedding in the dream, and Love—as everyone calls her—harbored a kind of obsessive fantasy about her own someday-in-the-future wedding.

"I dreamed about this story of a wedding planner who falls in love with the groom at one of her weddings," Love later recalled of her inspirational night vision. "It was a strange dream, but when I woke up the next morning I thought it was a great idea for a movie."

Love should know what makes for an appealing story line. As the reigning teenage "It Girl" in Hollywood, the petite 20-year-old has captured audiences on both the big and the small screen. Love has costarred in the recent teen slasher megahits, *I Know What You Did Last Summer* and the sequel *I Still Know What You Did Last Summer*, as well as a handful of other movies popular with young viewers. On the sizzling-hot nighttime soap opera *Party of Five*, Love plays the well-liked character Sarah Reeves, a

Jennifer Love Hewitt models her "Pink Ladies" jacket at the opening night festivities of Hollywood's rerelease of Grease. *Hewitt has become the latest Hollywood "It Girl"—the center of media attention—with her success in television shows and movies, popular with young viewers.*

conflicted and inexperienced girl-next-door with a big heart. Sarah is a typical teen with some serious problems—like discovering that her parents never told her she was adopted—and plenty of everyday confusions, such as whether or not to have sex with her boyfriend.

Even Love can relate to Sarah. "I'm completely like Sarah in every way possible," she says. "Like in the first couple of episodes when she was chasing after Bailey [played by heartthrob Scott Wolf], those are totally the things that I would do and say. And all the embarrassing things she did as far as like being the klutz and everything, that is completely me," Love admits.

Fans feel like they know Jennifer Love Hewitt: the true-blue friend, the real-looking girl with straight brown hair and a warm smile, the down-to-earth pal who has everything going for her but is still a regular teen and a good person.

Yet Love does not lead an everyday life. Far from it! As a successful singer with three albums to her credit, and an up-and-coming actress with 10 movies plus a hit TV series, Jennifer Love Hewitt may look like the girl next door. But she's not—not unless you live in Hollywood, that is.

Love's Story

After awakening with what she calls "the warm and fuzzies" from her wedding dream, Love immediately grabbed some paper. Quickly sketching an outline of her dream, Love carefully fashioned it into a 10-page "treatment," or sales pitch for a film. She titled her screenplay proposal *Cupid's Love*, and immediately submitted it to the Writer's Guild—"with my check

The cast of Party of Five, *one of TV's most popular nighttime series. Front row, from left: Neve Campbell, Jacob Smith, Matthew Fox, Paula Devicq. Back row: Jeremy London, Lacey Chabert, Scott Wolf, Jennifer Love Hewitt.*

for $20," the actress recounted later. Then the nervous waiting began.

Love desperately wanted to star in the upbeat, romantic story she had created in her dream, and she fully intended to produce the movie herself. She had awesome visions of donning a breathtaking white gown as the cute young wedding planner who eventually gets to organize her own special day. It would be like experiencing a dream come true within a dream come true. But Love believed that, in reality, her chances were slim. "I was convinced they [the Hollywood executives] were going to laugh in my face," she admitted.

Love kept herself busy filming *I Still Know*, and dating her long-term beau Will Friedle, star of ABC-TV's hit series *Boy Meets World*. But, as her managers circulated her movie treatment throughout the studios, Love geared herself up for rejection.

To her amazement, the studio executives seemed interested—clearly wary of the too-young producer, but definitely curious. So Love began to make the rounds in Hollywood herself, spending a grueling week in angst-provoking meetings with some of the highest-ranking business executives in Tinseltown. Dressing for the part, Love wore a conservative business suit and wire-rimmed glasses—even though she does not usually wear suits or glasses. After all, Jennifer Love Hewitt is a successful actress. So, she acted . . . well, *mature*.

"It was incredibly nerve-wracking," Love complained later, once her tour through the lush, top-floor office suites of Hollywood had finally finished. About her first meeting with two top-dog New Line Cinema execs, the young actress imagined the worst possible outcome: "I thought it would be like, 'You're a 19-year-old who wants to come in here and have us give you millions of dollars to make a movie? Come back when you're 40.'" Love refused to let her fear get in the way of her vision, however. She explained later, "But I wasn't about to not try. I never want to be one of those people who complains about there not being any roles."

That's why Love visited every Hollywood executive who would see her, seeking out a savvy and daring studio willing to back a teenager's fantasy project. Then she resumed her nervous waiting, this time optimistically doubtful that her newest dream would ever come true.

In the meantime, the TV and film offers kept pouring in, so Love knew that she could continue to realize her other career goals. Jennifer Love Hewitt is not just a flavor-of-the-month. This is one young woman who makes her own dreams come true. The talented star made a life choice for herself—an ambitious path she has been on since she was very, very young.

2

LITTLE
LOVE SONGS

When Pat Hewitt was in college studying to become a speech pathologist, her best friend was a tall, lovely young woman named Love. At the time, Pat regarded her friend with the long blond hair, big blue eyes, and gorgeous figure as the most beautiful girl she had ever known. So Pat decided that, if she ever had a daughter, she would call her Love.

In 1970 Pat and her husband had their first child, a boy they named Todd. Eight years later Pat became pregnant again, this time with a girl. After Todd heard his mother's idea for his new baby sister's name, he announced that he thought Love was a weird name and that his new sibling might prefer a more "normal" one. Pat reconsidered and a compromise was reached in which Todd was allowed to select the new baby's first name. At the time, little Todd had a mad crush on a girl in the neighborhood who was named Jennifer, and so that is the name he chose.

On February 21, 1979, Jennifer Love Hewitt was born in a hospital in Waco, Texas. From the start, everyone called her Love. When she was only six months old, sadly,

Jennifer Love Hewitt can relate to all kinds of entertainers, such as this group from a local circus. When she was only a toddler, Love amazed her family with her love of performing. Early in her childhood, Love's mother knew that her daughter had the talent to be an entertainer—and a star.

Even as a toddler, Love often entertained her family and neighbors with her singing. A multi-talented teenager, she has also become a singer and songwriter who has released three successful albums.

her parents divorced, which was traumatic for the family.

Although Love's introduction to life may have been somewhat stressful and traumatic, her childhood was transformed into a story-book existence. Pat moved the family to Killeen, a small town north of Austin, Texas, where the children seemed to thrive in the safe and supportive community. Pat worked at an elementary school in the neighborhood, helping the local children with their speech problems, while Todd and Love attracted lots of friends with their outgoing personalities. As a toddler, Love often entertained at family and neighborhood gatherings with her singing and dancing. Smiling brightly, she often found herself the center of attention.

By the time Love was three years old, she had a new stepdad, Tom Dunn. A local entrepreneur, Dunn had swept Pat off her feet and quickly convinced her to marry him. After the wedding, he opened up what would prove to be a very successful custom t-shirt printing business, and the expanded family functioned as an integral part of the close-knit community of Killeen.

Special Love

"I thought everybody's little girl could do that," Love's mother said later about her toddler's remarkable ability to perform at parties and in public places. "But I soon realized that Jennifer definitely had something special."

Pat's realization became clear when Love was four, during a family dinner at a local supper club that featured a singer and a piano player. Pat freaked out when she noticed that her adventurous daughter was no longer at the dinner table, and she went dashing into an adjoining room after hearing what sounded like Love's high-pitched voice.

There sat little Love, perched confidently on top of the baby grand piano, singing her child-like version of "Help Me Make It Through the Night." Pat could not help but notice that the audience of diners was completely enthralled.

After the beaming little girl received a big round of applause, she got a sound scolding from her relieved mother. But Pat was also proud of her daughter, and she acknowledged the unmistakable truth: Love was destined to be a performer, perhaps even a star. The girl already had what it would take to be an entertainer, that is, the desire, a poised and charismatic personality, plus innate talent.

Pat enrolled Love in dance classes, where she enjoyed and excelled in tap, ballet, and modern jazz. By the time she was five years old, Love, too, knew that her future was in the entertainment industry. "I was inspired by the TV series *Punky Brewster* and the actress Soleil Moon Frye. I saw this little girl my age on television and thought, 'Well I could do that, too,'" she recalled years later.

While attending Belair Elementary School where her mother worked, Love took singing lessons as well as dance classes. At age six she had her performing debut—at a livestock show! "In the pig barn I sang Whitney Houston's 'The Greatest Love of All' and there was a talent scout there," the actress later remembered. Also memorable to her was the standing ovation she received after her performance.

The talent scout sought out Pat, expressing professional interest in Love and encouraging them to consider a move to Los Angeles. Pat was flattered, but the family chose to remain in Killeen so that the children could continue to enjoy the small-town and relatively stress-free environment. But Pat knew that a dramatic life change was in their future. It was obvious to all who knew the eager little performer that Love's destiny would unfold in front of a national, perhaps even an international, audience.

Starring Love

Love continued to sing and dance at live-stock shows, as well as at school functions and local telethons. When she was seven, Love transferred to Nolanville Elementary School, where her special talents were soon noted. "I remember that Christmas, I took the class on a field trip to a nearby mall," Freddie Harrell, Jennifer's second-grade teacher, still recalls. "And she went into one of these stores that had this booth that would allow you to make a video. When we got back to school, I ran the video she had made. She was singing and doing this dance. That's when I first became aware of how talented she was. There was this level of talent there that you just don't see in many seven-year-olds. It was the kind of thing you just don't forget."

When she was nine, Love entered a Texas beauty pageant and was awarded the "Living Doll" prize for her talent and poise. Soon after, the Texas Show Team contacted Pat to invite Love to join the traveling performance troupe. Pat decided that the opportunity to experience the sights and the people of Denmark and Russia, where the team would be on tour, would be a good education for her daughter.

It was during the Texas Show Team's overseas tour of autumn 1988, while Love entertained

When Love was nine she was selected to join the Texas Show Team, a traveling performance troupe, in an overseas tour. The team saw the sights in Russia, such as the river tour pictured here, and in Denmark. During that trip, Love realized that she wanted to make show business her career.

foreign audiences and explored the world outside of Killeen, that both Pat and Love made the same life-changing decision. "This is what my daughter should be doing with her life," Pat acknowledged while she listened from the wings to the thunderous applause that greeted Love's song and dance routines. "This is what I want to do," Love concluded as she smiled broadly from brightly lit stages halfway around the world.

The Big Move

When mother and daughter returned to Killeen shortly before Christmas, a family meeting was clearly necessary. Love felt ready to move to Los Angeles and embark on her professional career, but her family remained cautious and hesitant. The change would be enormous, impacting everyone's life, especially Love's. But the confident nine-year-old was determined to launch her career. "My mother told me, 'You know kids sometimes do things that they think they're going to be real good at, and if it doesn't go well, they grow up with all these awful psychological problems,'" Love recalls Pat warning her at the time. "But I begged her to let me try. My mom knew she didn't have a choice and that she might as well say okay."

Actually, the decision was a difficult one for everyone in the family. Todd, a senior in high school, would be uprooted at an awkward time. Pat would have to quit her job, relying on Tom's income from the t-shirt business to support the four of them. And Tom would be forced to remain behind in Texas so that he could continue to bring in the money they would need to get established in California.

Love's family finally decided they would take the risk and make the big move because they all believed so wholeheartedly in her talents and potential for stardom. Pat announced they would give Hollywood one month of their time. If Love failed to score some kind of decent-paying work in Hollywood, then they would simply return to Killeen after the 30-day trial.

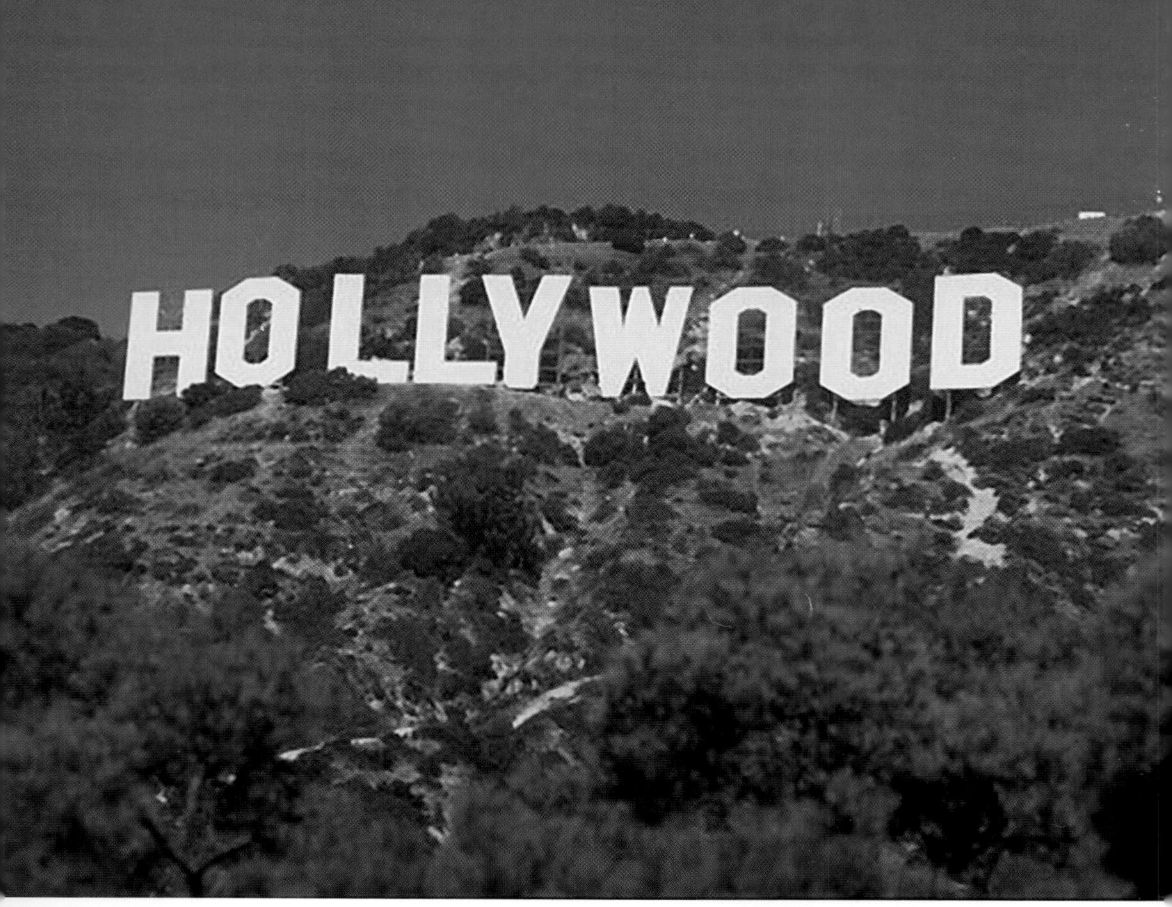
HOLLYWOOD

3

HOLLYWOOD
LOVE STORY

On February 21, 1989, Jennifer Love Hewitt celebrated her 10th birthday and her first day in Los Angeles, California. Pat, Todd, and Love had settled at the Oakwood Gardens Apartments, a rental community specially designed for aspiring child actors and their families. Love's new home was located right near the famous Hollywood sign and only a short drive away from many of the major motion picture and television studios.

On their second day in L.A., Pat and Love met with a talent agent interested in the little girl from Texas. "I said I wanted to be a great star who can sing, act, dance, and do everything," Love has said about her first meeting at a major Hollywood talent agency. "But other than that, I just want to be a normal little girl," she had boldly informed the agent. Within days, the agency signed Love on as a client and began sending her out on auditions.

Kids Incorporated

Although television roles for 10-year-olds were few and far between, especially for a new kid in town whose

---

Love's first day in Los Angeles was also her 10th birthday. Within weeks of the move to California—her home was only a short distance from the famous Hollywood sign—she had an agent and her first acting assignment.

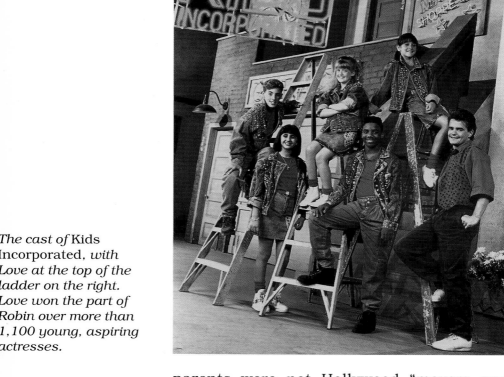

The cast of Kids Incorporated, *with Love at the top of the ladder on the right. Love won the part of Robin over more than 1,100 young, aspiring actresses.*

parents were not Hollywood "movers and shakers," Love's savvy agent was optimistic about the little girl's telegenic appearance and authentic, infectious personality. So Love was immediately sent to audition for a part in the frontline cast of the Disney Channel's *Kids Incorporated.*

More than 1,100 young hopefuls tried out for the role of Robin, one of the preteens who would sing, dance, and perform educational message-oriented skits in the popular show's sixth season. The producers and casting agents immediately warmed to Love, selecting her to return for additional auditions known as "callbacks," before finally casting her as Robin. In less than two weeks, Love had landed her first Hollywood gig.

Thousands of kids—and adults—flock to Hollywood every year to face repeated rejections (and heartbreak) in the cutthroat competition of casting calls—known in the business as "cattle calls." Few are selected to play small roles in obscure movies and television pilots. Fewer still are given the rare opportunity to become a screen actor. For most the depressing and energy-draining process requires years of dogged persistence. For Jennifer Love Hewitt, "making it" in L.A. occurred virtually overnight, her magical transformation from Texas talent to Hollywood TV star taking place in less than 30 days.

Love's first job turned out to be another Hollywood fantasy—"kind of like a dream come true" is how the actress has described her role as Robin on *Kids Incorporated.* She explained, "I loved to sing, loved to dance, and loved hanging out with people my own age, so it was a lot of fun."

Fun, and hard work: *Kids Incorporated* was a full-time job, so Love had to attend classes at a school for professional child actors in between rehearsals and time spent on the set. She also began appearing in television commercials—including 20 ads with Barbie for Mattel toys, plus ads for Circuit City, Chex cereals, and Mrs. Smith's pies. She toured the United States, Europe, and Asia with a group of talented kids who performed at trade shows, a trip sponsored by L.A. Gear sportswear. By the end of her first year in Los Angeles, Love was earning a better-than-decent living as a performer. She had proven herself to be true Hollywood talent.

Tom sold his t-shirt business and joined the family in L.A. And, in the fall of 1990, Love left the actors' school to enroll in a Los Angeles junior high in a further attempt to preserve her self-image as a "normal little girl."

"I got the feeling that I never really fit in when I was in Texas," Love has stated about her earliest years. "I would host, direct, and star in all these little plays at school and things and none of my friends really wanted to do it." Public school in California proved to be even more alienating. "My teachers said that I was ruining my life because I was acting, and that I was going to end up stupid because I wasn't going to have a good education. Yet, I had traveled the world, I had social skills, and I was an A student," Love has complained.

Fitting in with her classmates was extremely difficult for Love. "The other kids thought I was a nerd," she now admits sadly. "In their eyes I was weird because I acted, did things differently, and didn't go to parties. The kids just thought I was some kind of freak and would sometimes try to beat me up. I used to get soda poured on me and all kinds of awful things."

Although she was either ridiculed or ignored in school, on the set of *Kids Incorporated* Love felt comfortable and accepted. During the three years she played Robin, Love was regularly featured as the lead singer and dancer. Before the eyes of her growing following of fans, Jennifer Love Hewitt evolved into a polished performer.

Love Songs

In 1991, Love sang "Please Save Us the World" in a *Kids Incorporated* skit about cleaning up the environment. The pop ballad was a big hit and became the theme song for the show.

Later that year Love was sent with a group of young celebrities to perform the *Kids* song at the Earth Summit global environmental conference held in Rio de Janeiro, Brazil. The experience was thrilling for Love, who hoped also to become known as a professional singer and songwriter.

After singing, dancing, and exercising her way through a 20-minute kids' aerobics video called *Dance! Workout with Barbie*, Love received an exciting offer from her agent. The Japanese recording label Medlac Records was interested in turning the gifted young singer into a pop star sensation in Europe and Asia.

In 1992 Jennifer Love Hewitt's first album was released. *Love Songs* featured "Please Save Us the World," the *Kids Incorporated* anthem, along with other rocking ballads—including "Bedtime Stories," written by pop star Debbie Gibson, who also sang backup vocals on the track. Love was especially proud of the song she cowrote called "'90s Kids."

The first single off Love's album, "Dance with Me," quickly rose to the top of the Japanese dance charts, remaining in the number-one slot for four weeks. Love toured Japan to promote the record, reveling in her fame as a pop star. Singles off the album also hit the charts in England, Austria, Switzerland, and Germany, but *Love Songs* was never released in the United States.

Back in America, Love enthused about her

While she was working on Kids Incorporated, *Love enrolled in a public junior high school. However, it was hard for the bright, outgoing girl to fit in with her classmates, who saw her as different because of her acting career.*

A busy sidewalk music store in Japan. The first single on Love's debut album, "Dance with Me," immediately went to the top of the Japanese dance charts and stayed at number one for four weeks. In 1992 Love toured Japan to promote the record.

first record tour: "I had a great time performing in Japan. I felt like I was sort of in my own little world. I was as tall as everyone in the country. It was just so cool!"

Not yet 13, Jennifer Love Hewitt was already a celebrity, a TV star, and an international performer. Her three-year stint as Robin on *Kids Incorporated* complete, the teenager began to focus on a bigger dream: the silver screen.

Little Miss Movies

Munchie is the tale of a magical little alien creature who fights modern-day schoolyard bad guys and brings together two preteens in their first romance. The competition for the film's lead female role was stiff, but writer-director Jim Wynorski selected Love to play the part of Andrea. "She just stood out," Wynorski explained later. "Love just had this unbelievable willingness to perform."

And unbelievable luck!

Love was ecstatic about her first film role, and she handled the hectic 18-day shooting schedule (and mature scenes as a romantic partner to the male lead) like a real pro. According to the director, Love was perfectly cast. "She was able to project the necessary elements of being cute and spunky real well. It also helped that the whole cast just loved her and that she got along well with everybody."

Wynorski responded to the film reviewers' enthusiasm for Love by creating another kids' film, this time writing it specifically for the young actress. "I decided to write *Little Miss Millions* as a heavy drama that would give her a lot to do. I had such a good time writing it that I decided to just call Love straightaway and offer her the part."

Love was asked to star as Heather Lofton, a rich 12-year-old girl on the run from her wicked, money-grubbing stepmother in a desperate attempt to locate her real mother. Heather is plucky, funny, smart, and sweet, so Love adored the role and agreed to do *Little Miss Millions*. Pat even consented to be in the film in a small nonspeaking part, appearing as a secretary in one scene.

By the time *Little Miss Millions* was shown on television and released to video in 1993, Love had become a bankable screen actress. Her agent was fielding a variety of offers as Love's career began to bud and bloom—on a number of media branches. Jennifer Love Hewitt had plenty of career paths she could take. As usual, she followed her dreams—straight to success.

4

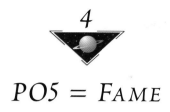

PO5 = FAME

Since arriving in California, Pat had been employed as a speech pathologist, but she was spending more and more of her time on sets and in business meetings with Love. When Love was 13 and her agent suggested that they look for teenage roles rather than the kids' parts she had been playing, Pat decided it was time to quit her job and focus full-time on managing Love's career. She wanted to ensure that her teenager stayed on track—and out of the fast lane. Hollywood has always been an easy place to lose focus and get into trouble, especially when your body is rapidly maturing and your hormones are raging.

Love appreciated her mother's selfless devotion. "She works really hard to make sure I'm taken care of," the young actress commented on Pat's choice to give up her own career for her daughter's. "But the best part is the idea that I have my best friend and confidante with me all the time."

Pat and Love agreed that a role in a television series would be a stable job and a wise career move. Desirable

---

The cast of the 1992–93 TV series Shaky Ground, *with Love Hewitt on the right. The series was 13-year-old Love's first chance to play a teenager rather than a child.*

parts for teenagers in Hollywood movies are less readily available than children's roles, so when the new Fox television sitcom *Shaky Ground* offered Love the chance to play Bernadette Moody, the Hewitts immediately signed on.

Love enjoyed playing the Moody family's brilliant young daughter, who was fresh, precocious, and very quick with the one-liners. Unfortunately, with the show running in a time slot opposite *60 Minutes,* the audience was limited. After only 17 episodes, *Shaky Ground* was canceled. Love felt tremendously disappointed, and she discovered for the first time what it would be like to be without a gig in Hollywood. "I learned that just because I had a job and was somewhat successful didn't mean that I was anything more than a working actor," she confided to a journalist at the time. "I realized that at any time I could not get the next job and not be working for months and months. I wouldn't be a star. I would just be an out-of-work actor." It was a humbling feeling. Fortunately for Love, the situation proved to be very temporary.

Back in the Act

Offered the opportunity to appear with long-time favorite Whoopi Goldberg and newcomer Lauryn Hill in a sequel to the box office hit *Sister Act,* Love quickly returned to work. Her first big-budget movie produced by a major Hollywood studio—*Sister Act II: Back in the Habit*—allowed Love to demonstrate her budding talents as a young adult actress. And in the role of the rap-loving choir girl Margaret, Love was also able to sing and dance in the film. She loved the entire process. "Making movies for me is still like living in the middle of a dream," she gushed.

For the first time in her short career, Love billed herself under her full name, appearing in the credits as Jennifer Love Hewitt. Up until *Sister Act II*, she had been using Love Hewitt as her professional name, since that was what everyone called her. "I had never made a conscious decision to omit Jennifer from my name," she explained years later. But, at 14, to go by her full given name "suddenly just seemed like the right thing to do."

After a guest role as ditsy Jennifer Love Fetterman on *Boy Meets World*—where she first met one of the cute stars of the popular series, Will Friedle—Love was invited to costar in a new television drama on ABC. As the rebellious 15-year-old Franny, Love spent the first eight months of 1994 on location in Hawaii filming *The Byrds of Paradise*, and she received her first on-screen kiss. "I had never kissed anybody before in my whole life and I was scared half to death," Love admitted afterward. But a bit of practice in the bushes with her 19-year-old costar served to ease Love's awkwardness and instantly erased her fears.

Despite critical success, poor ratings forced *The Byrds* off the air in mid-season. Love soon accepted another role of a rebellious teen on yet another short-lived dramatic series, ABC's *McKenna*. The show was filmed in the great wilderness of Oregon, and the adventurous part of young Cassidy McKenna enabled Love to try out such risky stunt work as rock climbing and white-water rafting.

Love began to panic, however, when the show was canceled after a brief run. Just 16, Love had already starred in three canceled television shows in as many years. Might it not be better to prevent future disappointment by turning down all subsequent offers to act in a television series?

Party Time

Love returned to Los Angeles to focus on her songwriting and singing, since she had already signed a recording contract with Atlantic Records and needed to put together her song list. So she was quite busy and happy when the fax arrived one day, followed by a package with a thick script bearing an unfamiliar abbreviation: PO5.

"I thought, 'What's PO5?'" Love has recalled about her blasé attitude when she first held what was to become her future, her big Hollywood break, in her hands. "I didn't have a clue." PO5, it turned out, was Fox's young nighttime drama *Party of Five.*

The Fox series, which has been dubbed "the thinking person's soap" and "prime time's classiest drama," was struggling into its second season. Not yet a hit, the sincere and message-oriented show aimed at twentysomethings had been grouped by critics—along with *ER* and *NYPD*—as part of "the bold new wave of TV dramas." It had also been compared to the '80s underground favorite *Thirtysomething*, this time an angst-ridden series written specifically for Generation Xers.

Young people, including lots of teenagers, loved the show, but the viewer base was not large enough to boost *PO5*'s ratings. When rumors circulated that the series would end after the first season, over 15,000 fans wrote to request that Fox keep *PO5* on the air. The ratings began a slow climb, and 28,000 viewers voted to send the series into its second

season in *TV Guide's* annual "Save Our Show" poll in the spring of 1995. When *PO5* returned to the air in the fall, it was the lowest-rated prime-time series on a major network to be renewed.

The series' coproducers were all too aware of the fact that *PO5* needed to attract a lot more viewers to remain on the air. So in order to increase audience appeal, they made sure that the *Party* scripts got steamier. This meant that more love interests for the main characters needed to be hired. When the character of Sarah Reeves was created as a flame for one

Love's on-screen relationship with Party of Five's *Scott Wolf (pictured here) is very complex and sometimes difficult. Off-screen, however, Wolf, Hewitt, and other members of the cast tell jokes, have fun, and always enjoy each other's company while working on the set.*

of the main characters, 17-year-old Bailey Salinger, Jennifer Love Hewitt was asked to audition for the part.

The series' primary story line focuses on the Salinger family, five orphaned children living in San Francisco who lost their parents in a car accident in the show's first season. The oldest, Charlie (Matthew Fox), is an irresponsible and moody womanizer. Reluctantly he runs the family business and heads the family —and falls in love with his siblings' nanny, Kirsten Bennett (Paula Devicq). Teenagers Bailey (Scott Wolf) and Julia (Neve Campbell) help out with 11-year-old Claudia (Lacey Chabert) and baby Owen. They spend most of their time, however, discussing and trying to deal with serious, but not uncommon, crises— including drunken mishaps, drug abuse, casual sex and infidelity—while bouncing in and out of crushes and relationships. After his girlfriend dies of a drug overdose, Bailey turns to his true-blue, straight-as-an-arrow friend Sarah Reeves for comfort, and the flame is ignited.

When Love first read the script for *PO5*, she felt an immediate rapport with Sarah: "I was like, 'Wow, This character talks exactly like me!' I knew how to play her instantly." So, Love auditioned as herself—in jeans and a t-shirt with very little makeup. And it worked. It worked so well, in fact, that the producers altered the storyline for Sarah Reeves, custom-tailoring the scripts to fit Love's own personality. Plus, they expanded her role from a small, guest spot scheduled for a handful of episodes into a full-time part on the show. "Love is [an] example of an actor who came to the show and you waited to see

how she fit into the family and what she could do as an actor," reports *PO5*'s coexecutive producer Amy Lippman. "As soon as we saw her (Love) in action, we knew we wouldn't let go of her ever, ever, ever."

Love has long days on the set of PO5, *which begin at 6 A.M. with hair and makeup and often do not end before 8 P.M.*

Party Girl

As the show's ratings climbed steadily, Love settled into her complicated, on-screen relationship with Scott Wolf's Bailey. Female fans who were Wolf worshipers felt angry at first, resentful toward newcomer Love. Many wrote letters to complain of their disappointment that their favorite hunky teen character—who, in real life, is 10 years older—seemed to have settled down. "I get a lot of hate mail about that," Love stated in 1996.

Yet Love knew she was in the role of a life-time. As she informed *People* magazine, "Some-times I say, 'Wow, I'm the luckiest teenager alive—kissing an older man every day *and* getting paid for it!'"

A typical day on the set of *PO5* begins at 6 A.M. with hair and makeup, and it does not end before 8 P.M. Filmed largely in L.A., the show is in production five days a week for nine months out of the year. Fortunately the dedicated ensemble (or multi-member) cast enjoys one another as much as their work. They play pranks, tell jokes, and generally have lots of fun on the set. As Neve Campbell once told the press, "We all hit it off really, really well." And the close-knit cast had welcomed Love into the group right away. "She's really sweet and talented," says Scott Wolf, who had guest-starred with Love on *Kids Incorporated* back in 1991. "It's brought a nice warmth to the set."

The role of Sarah Reeves was not the usual teen character part, and it varied considerably from Love's previous fresh-mouthed rebel-kid roles. Love was intrigued that playing Sarah would not be pretending to be some adult's version of a one-dimensional teenager, but rather she would be portraying a real young person a lot like herself. "She's a cool person. She's not the typical teenager they put on tele-vision who is obsessed with sex and partying," Love says about Sarah, sounding as if she is talking about herself. "Sarah's in school, she's smart, and she has a good head on her shoulders. She's stupid sometimes and she can make mistakes. In other words she's human."

Love, too, was still attending school, using

Love celebrates the release of her second album, Let's Go Bang. The CD was popular enough on the international market for Atlantic Records to plan a follow-up album.

tutors, and taking correspondence courses. She was earning straight As, which she somehow managed to achieve while mastering her new full-time *PO5* job and putting the finishing touches on her second album. Only two weeks after she premiered in the second season opener of *Party of Five*, Love's first American release hit the airwaves.

Let's Go Bang ("bang" meaning a certain type of dance) is a lively mix of fun and funky dance tracks and love songs, including the bluesy single "Couldn't Find Another Man" and a ballad, "Free to Be a Woman," cowritten by Love. The critics' quick dismissal of *Let's Go Bang* was disappointing to Love, and she admitted that the album's sexy-sounding title was probably a mistake. However, the record was popular internationally and with Love's large following of fans, Atlantic was satisfied enough to sign her on for a follow-up album.

In the meantime, *Party of Five* was captivating an increasing number of faithful viewers. As her character confronted new challenges and shared raw emotions each week on *PO5*, Love's fan mail began to change, and multiply. After the episode in which Sarah Reeves discovers that she is adopted, bags of letters addressed to Love (or to Sarah) were stacked up at the Fox offices. Adopted children bared their souls in long letters to Love, sharing their own experiences and private feelings. Love was also receiving loads of mail from kids who had problems with their parents, and from boys who were admittedly smitten with the young actress.

Midway through her first season on *PO5*, Love experienced her first off-screen romance. Like Love, 20-year-old Joey Lawrence had been a child star, a regular on TV's *Gimme a Break* during the 1980s and *Blossom* in the '90s. The relationship was brief and casual, however, and the two busy actors soon separated. "The polite way of putting it is that the business got the better of our relationship," is how Love has explained the young couple's quick breakup.

Pat continued to supervise her daughter's escalating career, holding the teenager to a strict 10 P.M. curfew and urging her daughter to take the time to relax, chill out, and have some fun. Pat agreed to allow Love to host two somewhat educational specials on MTV—*True Tales of a Teen Trauma* and *True Tales of a Teen Romance,* and advised her when, during the 1996 summer break from *PO5,* the movie offers flooded in. "I like having my mom around," 17-year-old Love genuinely conceded. "I still need my mom."

5

TEEN SCREAM QUEEN

ove planned to focus all of her energy on the development of her third record album during her first summer break from *Party of Five*, but a film offer came in that was too exciting to turn down. *House Arrest*, which stars Jamie Lee Curtis and Jennifer Tilly, is a thoughtful comedy about kids who lock their folks in the basement together after the parents announce their intention to divorce. Love was interested in the part of Brooke Figler, a popular 13-year-old beauty.

When the movie's producer expressed concern that 17-year-old Love looked too mature for the role of Brooke, the actress showed up for her callback (second audition) without makeup on, her long straight hair styled in girlish curls. And she acted somewhat immature. Love won the part.

Despite her demanding schedule, the young actress was ecstatic. "The movie was an absolute blast!" Love enthused after the filming was completed. "I got to work with great actors and to play a great character in an entertaining story. And the highlight for me was I got to

Love Hewitt (top left) with the cast of House Arrest. *The film not only gave Love the chance to work with stars Jamie Lee Curtis and Jennifer Tilly, it also allowed her to sing a song that later would be included in her new album.*

sing a song, 'It's Good to Know [That] I'm Alive,' which is going to be on my new album. I also got my second screen kiss."

Love in Love

Before *PO5* resumed filming, Love found the time to appear in yet another movie, and to receive her third big-screen kiss. The Warner Bros. film *Trojan War* stars Will Friedle as the love-struck Bradley, with Love as his best friend, Leah. Practical, reliable Leah finds herself falling in love with Bradley once she realizes he's about to make love to another girl. After a comedic all-night romp—which features send-ups of other movies, including a speeding bus scene and a hilarious homage to *Saturday Night Fever*—Leah finally gets her boy.

In real life, the same script for a friendship-to-love story was playing itself out.

Love had fallen for Will earlier, after a friend fixed them up on a blind date, but the good-looking young actor was dating around and the two failed to hook up again. While shooting *Trojan War*—which focuses on Bradley's desperately silly attempts to obtain protection in order to practice safe sex with the bad girl of his dreams (played by Marley Shelton)—Will and Love became close friends. During their kissing scene at the end of the movie, Love knew she had a crush on her costar.

She expressed her romantic feelings first, when it seemed as if Will would never ask her out on a date. Eventually, the tight friendship turned romantic as the couple spent all their free time together, hanging out and doing simple things like shopping or going to McDonald's for Happy Meals.

But Love's free time was very limited. The

In the 1996 film Trojan War, Love played Leah, who falls in love with her best friend, played by Will Friedle. Off-screen the couple's relationship also started out as friendship and later turned into romance.

third season of *PO5* required a return to her full-time job, plus she was working hard to finish high school and to complete all of the promotion for her new album. When *Jennifer Love Hewitt* was released in September of 1996, Love's youthful and spirited music was once again extremely popular with her huge fan following in Europe and Asia.

Sarah Reeves was forced to do a lot of growing up on the 1996–97 season of *Party of Five*, adjusting to Bailey's college status and sexy female roommate, then confronting him when his partying evolves into alcoholism. After a drunken car accident in which Sarah is nearly killed, Bailey finally agrees to get help. With the scripts more focused on Sarah and Bailey than in the previous season, the series' ratings leapt dramatically to an all-time high. *PO5* even earned top honors, winning the Golden Globe Award as TV's Best Drama in 1996. And Love moved into the spotlight, becoming the latest star to emerge from the ultra-hot cast of *Party of Five*.

Love Screams

In the spring of 1997, Love was certainly living a dream life. Barely 18, her on-screen career was already a success, she was dating a sweet and adorable fellow actor, and she still had time to pen the love songs she so enjoyed writing. So, when the script arrived for a teen horror movie to be filmed that summer, Love really did not need to read it. She hated scary movies and, in fact, had never gone to one. "I don't like horror films," she admitted candidly to *Seventeen* magazine. "I wouldn't even watch them when I was growing up. But I've always told myself that I have to face up to what scares me."

I Know What You Did Last Summer intrigued the daring actress, and she forced herself to read the entire script. The screenplay had been written by Kevin Williamson, the screenwriter for *Scream*, the hit film that turned *PO5*'s Neve Campbell into a movie star. As Julie, one of four teens stalked by a mysterious man with a huge fishhook, Love's role would be both frighteningly large—she would appear in almost every scene—and nightmarish to play. The film was to be shot mostly at night, with the creepy stalker, gruesome murders, and blood-curdling screams dominating most scenes.

To her surprise, Love discovered she really wanted the role. And, true to form, the gifted actress got the part.

The young cast included Freddie Prinze Jr., Ryan Phillippe, and *Buffy the Vampire Slayer*'s Sarah Michelle Gellar. Everyone bonded while away on location in Wilmington, North Carolina, and, according to Prinze, the four quickly became "a team, a family." To prepare for their roles, they watched videos of horror movies together, including *The Shining, Scream*, and *Friday the 13th*, but Love admits she kept her eyes covered for much of the gore.

During filming, however, the character Julie could not shy away from the cold, dark, scary nights of *Last Summer*. Love did her own stunts and spent much of her on-screen time running and screaming. She surprised herself by both conquering her fears and having a lot of fun while filming the bloody thriller.

When the filming was over, Love was proud of herself. "It felt great," she said about playing the lead in a teen horror movie, "and the thought of actually doing my first leading role had me close to tears a lot of times. I've

A scene from I Know
What You Did Last
Summer. *From left:
Freddie Prinze Jr., Hewitt,
Sarah Michelle Gellar,
and Ryan Phillippe. Love
had previously avoided
horror films, finding them
too scary, but she over-
came her fears and had a
wonderful time working
on the movie.*

always dreamed about what it was going to be
like. The fact that it's finally happened is like
'Oh my God!'"

"Oh my God" was definitely right! When it
was released in October, 1997, *I Know What
You Did Last Summer* was an immediate box-
office smash, grossing more than $103 million
in the United States alone, before going worldwide and eventually being released on video.
Critics praised the hooking slasher flick as "a
crisply efficient thriller" and "a screamingly

good time." And suddenly Jennifer Love Hewitt was a big-screen superstar.

Loving Life

In June of 1997, Love had graduated from Laurel Springs High in Ojai, California, with the senior class of correspondent students. Although her top college choices included California's Pepperdine and Stanford Universities, as well as Boston University (the school she attends in *I Know What You Did Last Summer*), Love had chosen to return to the fourth season of *Party of Five* in the fall, putting her desire to study journalism and creative writing on hold. "I was really good in school," Love told *Cosmopolitan* magazine about earning her diploma in the midst of budding stardom. "I've always wanted to go to college, and I probably will in a couple of years. My college fantasy is sitting underneath a tree on campus with my glasses on and having a cool guy friend study with me, but he's just a friend—you know, that college thing where he becomes a friend for life."

Although her relationship with Will was still going strong, Love, at 18, had no plans for marriage. At least, not yet. "It's not like I'm afraid of commitment," the actress explained. "I've been making wedding plans since I was 12 years old and I read all the bridal magazines every month. . . . At this point Will and I are just enjoying being in love and being happy. We're both a little too busy to be talking about that stuff."

As if a full-time job in television was not keeping her busy enough, Love dove into an against-type part as Deb Friedman, an annoying airhead in the small independent film, *Telling You.* Somehow balancing her *PO5* filming

Love won the part of homecoming queen Amanda (as seen here with costar Ethan Embry) in the film Can't Hardly Wait. *In real life, however, Love had never been to a junior high or high school party with people her own age.*

with time spent on movie sets, Love soon scored the coveted part of shy homecoming queen Amanda in the high school party movie, *Can't Hardly Wait.*

"I've never been to a high school or a junior high school party with people my own age," Love had once admitted in *TV Guide.* In *Can't Hardly Wait,* she portrays with painfully realistic awkwardness the lack of self-confidence teens can feel when partying among their equally insecure peers. "She was the only person we went to for the role," bragged the popular comedy's executive producer Jenno Topping.

It was clear that Love had suddenly become one of the most sought-after young actresses in

Hollywood. She had enthusiastically signed on to star in the sequel to *I Know What You Did Last Summer*, and additional lucrative movie offers were piling up. Her newfound box-office clout allowed her to demand as much as $2 million per picture. And, although she had no desire to leave her full-time gig on *Party of Five*, Love knew that she had totally fallen in love with making movies.

Love began to toy with the idea of creating her own movies. In the spring of 1998, after a typically hectic Hollywood day, Love fell asleep one night. And she had a strangely wonderful dream—about weddings.

6

LOVE
CONQUERS ALL

While she waited to hear whether any of the major
movie studios were willing to take a risk on a 19-
year-old producer with a wedding obsession, Love went
to work on her curvy but petite, 5' 3" body. She adopted a
special protein diet, sweated through aerobics, and
trained with weights in preparation for the filming of
I Still Know What You Did Last Summer, this time ready-
ing herself physically as well as psychologically for the
rigorous shooting schedule. Love knew that, once again,
there would be lots of action—constant scenes of running
away, exhausting attempts at fighting off the berserk
butcher with the ice hook—so she got in shape for the
stunt work. She readied her voice for continual screaming, while preparing a song for the soundtrack, "How Do
I Deal."

The hit horror sequel shoot turned out to be even more
demanding than expected. The scenes shot in the thick,
insect-infested mango orchards of Mexico were especially
horrific. "At any given time, you'd have 15 of them crawling

---

*Love, Brandy, and Jennifer Esposito in a scene from the 1998
horror sequel,* I Still Know What You Did Last Summer. *In
preparation for her demanding role in the movie, Love went into
training—both physically, for the action shots, and vocally, for
her character's constant screaming.*

on all different parts of your body—up your pants, in your shirt, on your head," Love later told of the buggy film set. "I even got one on my tongue in the middle of a scream."

The actress also lost her voice twice while screeching her way through a steady stream of bloody slasher attacks. But she had a great time reuniting for Nintendo matches with buddy Freddie Prinze Jr., and befriending fellow pop singer Brandy, who plays against type as a tough-talking tease. Love was even asked to provide input on the script, advising the film's producer to focus on Julie's emotional instability, a realistic result of all of the traumatic events that had taken place in the first movie. "I didn't want the audience to watch the lead character do the same things over and over because there's no fun in that," Love explained about the paranoia incorporated into the storyline for the justifiably troubled Julie.

Audiences watched *I Still Know* in absolute horrified glee, and the psycho-thriller film sequel brought in a respectable $39 million when it opened in the United States, earning millions more overseas and as a video. Critics took note of Love's physical screen presence: "Hewitt, especially, looks as if she could fend [the stalker] off with a quick flex of her abs. It's not just her body that's sculpted and toned: her entire personality seems aerobicized." Before audiences had ample time to recover, another sequel was rumored to be in the works—with Love signed on once more.

New Hooks

In the meantime, New Line Cinema grabbed up Love's story idea for *Cupid's Love*, retitling it *Marry Me Jane*, and Columbia Pictures offered Love a deal to produce more films in the future. "She's an absolute powerhouse," stated Columbia's admiring president, Amy Pascal. "She's always so together."

Love had to be, with the incredible schedule she was facing in the fall of 1998. In addition to filming her fourth season on *Party of Five*, the "powerhouse" actress was: $500,000 richer for her story idea and on the fast track at New Line as executive producer and star of *Marry Me Jane*; playing a music industry executive in the Ben Stiller comedy, *The Suburbans*; starring in an ABC movie, a biography of the late screen star, Audrey Hepburn; and taping a pilot for her own TV series, a spinoff from *PO5* focusing on Sarah Reeves.

"She demands to be taken seriously at a very young age," remarked another top production executive at Columbia, Matt Tolmack, of the Hollywood mini-industry known as Jennifer Love Hewitt.

Love agrees. That is why she has thoughtfully and carefully adjusted her on-screen image. Her planned transition was to mature suddenly from sweetheart teen to wholesome adult, and occasional sex symbol (but never unclothed). Love has turned down seductive roles that would require nudity. She doesn't drink, smoke, or spend time around people who do. As a serious young adult, Love's real-life image is as squeaky clean as the characters she plays on screen— grown-up and attractive, but morally straight.

For *Marry Me Jane*, Love will be playing a marriage-minded woman, while at the same time she will be doubling behind the camera in the very adult role of executive producer.

In *The Suburbans*, an ensemble comedy-drama about an '80s New Wave band that reunites after wasting away their brief fame and big fortune, Love struts her grown-up stuff as Cate Phillips, a record industry talent agent who masterminds the group's second chance at glory.

Her role as Audrey Hepburn in the ABC biopic, developed by Pulitzer prize-winning playwright Marsha Norman, requires Love to fill the glass slippers of one of America's most loved princesses of the silver screen.

"The most amazing part will be getting to wear her clothes," an awestruck Love told *Cosmopolitan* magazine about the fashion trendsetter known for her cool capri pants, dark glasses, and simple shifts. Long infatuated with the star of such film classics as *Breakfast at Tiffanys* (1961) and *My Fair Lady* (1964), Love enjoyed studying one of her big movie idols. And she was surprised to find out that she could really identify with Hepburn as a woman: "Especially her insecurity. I'm the most insecure person on the planet, but it helps keep me grounded," Love has admitted.

Love's two-year romance also proved to be less secure than she had hoped. She split up with Will Friedle in the midst of the chaotic whirlwind that accompanied her rise to superstardom and selection as Hollywood's youngest new "It Girl." She remains friendly with Will, however, and characteristically optimistic about her romantic future. "I've had my wedding planned since I was 12," Love has revealed. "I have one planned for winter, fall, spring, and summer—depending on when it is—with the seating arrangements and everything. I think I'm going to be one of those people who marries young, like 23, 24, just because it's always been my dream."

Audrey Hepburn, in her famous role as Eliza Dolittle in My Fair Lady. *Love was thrilled to be chosen to portray Hepburn, one of her screen idols, in a 1999 ABC film biography.*

A dream Love will now be able to at least practice living out in her own dream-come-true movie. *Marry Me Jane* is scheduled to begin shooting in mid-1999 when Love is between seasons for *Party of Five*.

The Time of Her Life

In the meantime, Love began dating MTV-deejay Carson Daly, the hip host of *Total*

Request Live. "She's everything I've ever looked for in a girl. She's perfect," pronounced the smitten Daly in the spring of 1999.

If she's perfect, Love doesn't know it. She may be a Hollywood powerhouse with millions of fans, but Jennifer Love Hewitt is no prima donna. She's friendly, she's as real in person as she appears on the screen, and she's every bit a star-struck American woman.

Love's big-time crush on the darkly handsome actor Johnny Depp, for example, is no secret. However, when Depp turned up on the set of *Party of Five* one day to say hello to one of his most enthusiastic, and most famous, fans, Love freaked out. She wasn't wearing any makeup and felt totally ugly, so she ran screaming into the makeup trailer and locked herself in. When Love graduated from high school, the thoughtful Depp sent flowers.

Like most people her age, Love loves junk food, especially mushroom pizza, cheeseburgers, french fries, and ice-cold Pepsi. She's more comfortable discussing boyfriends, clothes, and college plans than rattling off her movie grosses, television ratings, and power moves in Hollywood. She surfs, rollerblades to interviews with journalists, and sleeps with her teddy bears and a cluster of angel figurines nearby because, she claims, "they make you feel safe." And Love still lives with her mother.

In the summer of 1998, Love bought a spacious five-bedroom house in San Fernando Valley. Pat, who is divorced from Tom Dunn now, lives in the sunny downstairs rooms, while Love chills out upstairs with her two cats, Don Juan and Haylie. "We've never spent a night apart," Pat confides about her protective, nurturing relationship with Hollywood's sweetheart.

When Love was first moving furniture from the moving truck into the house, a youngster rode up on a bicycle. Spotting the TV star chatting with movers, the excited little girl shouted, "Oh my God! A celebrity is moving to my neighborhood!" Equally excited, Love looked up and down the street, then yelled back, "Oh my God, which house?"

Such is the real-person mentality of Jennifer Love Hewitt, a superstar who still acts like the girl-next-door. It is no wonder the 20-year-old is such a success as an actress, as the camera only serves to showcase Love's personality, her down-to-earth cuteness and innate sweetness.

However, as well as being a nice person, Love is also a savvy businesswoman. When *PO5* cocreators Christopher Keyser and Amy Lippman first proposed a spinoff series to Love, the poker-faced actress appeared unimpressed by the offer. But when Love's agent completed the negotiations for her client, the new star of *The Time of Your Life* was guaranteed a $1.3 million deal, plus a plum role as one of the series' producers.

The spinoff, which will be less dark and more comic in tone than *PO5*, focuses on Sarah Reeves's search for her birth father. In the series pilot, Sarah leaves behind Bailey, the Salingers, and San Francisco, setting off on her own for New York City. The series will premiere in the fall of 1999.

In addition to her busy TV and movie schedule, Love finds the time to film commercials. She is currently serving as an advertising spokeswoman for Neutrogena skin-care products and makeup and appears sporting a white mustache in the celebrity-studded ads from the National Milk Board.

Love is also learning to play the guitar and working on a fourth album, for which she has high hopes. In what little free time she has, Love writes poetry and volunteers for Tuesday's Child, a nonprofit organization that assists children with AIDS. She wrote a touching essay about time spent with one terminally ill child for the bestselling book *Chicken Soup for the Teenage Soul.*

Once asked if she thought that *Party of Five* was a good influence on kids, Love responded in the affirmative: "Absolutely. The media tend to make teenagers seem very stupid and unaware of what's going on around them, interested only in sex, drugs, and parties. The great thing about *Party of Five* is you have four or five teenagers on that show who are handling situations better than most 40-year-olds could ever dream to handle them."

The "great thing" about Jennifer Love Hewitt is that she, too, is handling a very challenging situation—superstardom—with a refreshing sense of responsibility and maturity. And she seems willing to confront and conquer her insecurities, sharing the process with appreciative audiences worldwide. "She is talented, beautiful, and sings like an angel," summarizes fellow actress Jamie Lee Curtis. "She has the tools to do whatever she wants."

What Love wants is to be happy in her personal life, and fulfilled as a creative artist and professional performer. Like most young people, she wants to live out her dreams. By working hard and taking risks, Jennifer Love Hewitt is doing just that. And in doing so, Love is serving as a remarkable role model for preteens, teenagers, and young adults, an

In addition to her work in films, TV, and music, Love finds time to volunteer in the community. Here, along with hundreds of other volunteers, she helps serve Thanksgiving meals to the homeless in Los Angeles.

inspiration to people of all ages, as a singer, actress, and all-around good person.

Love's star will undoubtedly continue to shine brightly, both in the studios of Hollywood and in her own dazzling dreams.

CHRONOLOGY

1979   Born Jennifer Love Hewitt on February 21 in Waco, Texas; parents divorce and family relocates to Killeen, Texas

1985   Begins performing at area livestock shows, telethons, and school functions; is noted by talent scouts

1988   Joins the Texas Show Team, touring the U.S., Russia, and Denmark

1989   Moves to Hollywood; lands role of Robin in TV series *Kids Incorporated*; appears in commercials; performs on tour for L.A. Gear

1991   Films workout video *Dance! Workout with Barbie*

1992   Records first album, *Love Songs*, for Japan's Medlac Records; acts in her first film, *Munchie*; lands role in TV series *Shaky Ground*

1993   Stars in children's film *Little Miss Millions;* appears in film *Sister Act II*

1994   Costars in television series *The Byrds of Paradise* and *McKenna*; signs a recording contract with Atlantic Records

1995   Cast as Sarah Reeves in Fox's *Party of Five*; releases album, *Let's Go Bang*

1996   Films *House Arrest* and *Trojan War;* begins dating Will Friedle; releases album, *Jennifer Love Hewitt*

1997   Plays lead in blockbuster *I Know What You Did Last Summer*

1998   Appears in indie film *Telling You;* costars in high school romp *Can't Hardly Wait*; plays lead in horror sequel *I Still Know What You Did Last Summer*; successfully pitches her own movie, *Marry Me Jane,* to New Line Cinema; breaks up with Friedle; begins dating MTV's Carson Daly

1999   Appears in adult comedy *The Suburbans*; films ABC's biopic about Audrey Hepburn; films pilot for *The Time of Your Life,* her own *Party of Five* spinoff show; wins Teen Choice Awards for Choice Actress in a Film and Female Hottie of the Year

FILMOGRAPHY

Feature Films

1992   *Munchie*

1993   *Little Miss Millions*
           Sister Act II: Back in the Habit

1996   *House Arrest*

1997   *Trojan War*
           I Know What You Did Last Summer

1998   *Telling You*
           Can't Hardly Wait
           I Still Know What You Did Last Summer

1999   *The Suburbans*
           Marry Me Jane (also executive producer)

Television Series

1989–91 *Kids Incorporated*

1992–93 *Shaky Ground*

1994   *The Byrds of Paradise*

1994–95 *McKenna*

1995–99 *Party of Five*

1999–   *The Time of Your Life*

TV Specials

1996   *True Tales of Teen Trauma* (MTV, host)
           True Tales of Teen Romance (MTV, host)

1997   *Senior Prom* (ABC, host)

1999   Untitled biopic about Audrey Hepburn (ABC movie)

DISCOGRAPHY

Albums

1992   *Love Songs* (Japan, Medlac)

1995   *Let's Go Bang* (Atlantic)

1996   *Jennifer Love Hewitt* (Atlantic)

Soundtracks

1996   "It's Good to Know That I'm Alive" (*House Arrest*)

1997   "I Believe In" and "I Hope I Don't Fall in Love with You" (*Trojan War*)

1998   "How Do I Deal" (*I Still Know What You Did Last Summer*)

Video

1991   *Dance! Workout with Barbie*

Writings

1997   "Bright Heart" in *Chicken Soup for the Teenage Soul*

FURTHER READING

Canfield, Jack, Mark Victor Hansen, and Kimberly Kirberger. *Chicken Soup for the Teenage Soul: 101 Stories of Life, Love and Learning.* Deerfield Beach, FL: Health Communications, Inc., 1997.

Golden, Anna Louise. *Jennifer Love Hewitt.* New York: St. Martin's Press, 1999.

Hensley, Dennis. "What's Not to Love?" *Cosmopolitan*, November, 1998.

Nerz, A. Ryan. *Scene: Jennifer Love Hewitt.* New York: Aladdin Paperbacks, 1997.

Noonan, Rosalind. *Party of Five—Sarah: Don't Say You Love Me.* New York: Pocket Books, 1998.

Party of Five (series of novels based on the show), New York: Pocket Books, 1997.

Royce, Brenda Scott. *Party of Five: The Unofficial Companion.* Los Angeles: Renaissance Books, 1997.

Shapiro, Marc. *Love Story: The Unauthorized Biography of Jennifer Love Hewitt.* New York: Berkley Boulevard Books, 1998.

ABOUT THE AUTHOR

VIRGINIA ARONSON is a professional writer and author of more than 20 books, including several young adult biographies. She is the author of *Venus Williams*, also in the *Galaxy of Superstars* series. She lives in South Florida with her writer husband and young son.

INDEX